Dedication

This book is dedicated to all persons of color that have experienced racism or colorism, because the color of their skin didn't blend in.

Being the new kid in class has been a very hard task. "Can I touch your hair?" is what the other kids always ask.

Nobody else looks like Tate, so she gets treated differently. It can be hard to make friends when you're an outsider instantly!

Most of the children don't talk to her just because the color of her skin doesn't blend in. Some of the children have asked her if she knows her dad, she told them yes. Then they asked if he's in jail, and she said, "No, I'm blessed."

Do you know your dad?

Anyone that thinks poorly of you because the color of your skin doesn't blend in needs to learn about racism and empathy. Having brown skin doesn't make you the enemy.

The next day at school the children were saying mean things about Tate's dark skin. But with a confident smile, she said to them, "I'm proud of my beautiful dark skin! With my confidence and dark skin, I'll always win!"

After talking to the student's, she felt very proud of herself for speaking up. She walked into the bathroom, looked in the mirror and stared at her reflection. She smiled and thanked God for her beautiful complexion.

 My name is *Tate Robertson*. As of 2021, I am a chemistry student at Dillard University, and I love my beautiful brown skin! However, I haven't always been able to say that. I grew up in a small town and went to schools with people that didn't look like me. As a darker-skinned black girl, it was hard for me to grasp the fact that I was simply different from my peers, and it was even harder to become ok with the fact that I was seen as different, and that would never change. Hearing, "Why can't your hair get wet?" or "We can't see you" when the lights are out in class deeply affected how I saw myself. I would sit and wonder why I couldn't go play at some of my friends' houses. As I grew older, I wondered why I wasn't pretty enough to have a date to dances. Through the years, I've learned to love how my hair coils up when wet and that my skin tone deepens in the sun. I hope when anyone of color read this book, they will realize how beautiful brown is and that people of a different skin color deserve love and respect.

Made in the USA
Middletown, DE
02 February 2022

At the age of 21, Franklin C. Edwards (Frank) wrote and published his first children's book, Franklin the Helper – Just Be Yourself, as part of the Franklin the Helper collection. Frank hails from Houston, Texas, where he graduated high school and enrolled in college majoring in Business Administration. Frank was reared in the Baptist church and is guided by his Christian faith. He loves playing basketball, reading, recording music and spending time with his family and close friends.

As a youth, Frank enjoyed the work of Jeff Kinney (Diary of a Wimpy Kid series) and Masashi Kishimoto (Naruto series) and has always loved to read and write. Frank volunteered in his community as a youngster and participated in several youth programs. Those activities have given Frank the real-life knowledge and experiences he writes about in his children's books. These experiences motivate him with an empathetic heart to encourage children through the stories in his books. Frank has collaborated with a nonprofit organization, Students Combating Bullying Connection, Inc. and together, this team has reached and encouraged a large number of children utilizing Franklin the Helper.

The collection is written in rhyme to capture audiences and focuses on real-life situations that are relatable to youth. Frank has successfully blended his passion for writing rhymes and encouraging children through Franklin the Helper. Franklin the Helper is a friend to all. He is always ready to sit by his friend's side with great advice to provide!

Follow Franklin the Helper's new releases and great advice via the Students Combating Bullying Connection, Inc. website at www.scbconnection.org.